SERIES EDITOR: DONALD SOMMER

**OSPREY MODELLING MANUA**

# Supermarine Spitfire

RODRIGO HERNÁNDEZ CABOS AND GEOFF COUGHLIN

OSPREY
MODELLING

First published in Great Britain in 2001 by Osprey Publishing, Elms Court, Chapel Way, Botley, Oxford OX2 9LP United Kingdom
Email: info@ospreypublishing.com

ISBN 1 84176 266 0

Editor: Donald Sommerville
Design: Compendium Publishing Ltd

Originated by Accion Press
Printed in China through World Print Ltd

 02  03  04  05  10  9  8  7  6  5  4  3  2  1

**For a Catalogue of all books published by Osprey Military and Aviation please write to:**
The Marketing Manager, Osprey Publishing Ltd., P.O. Box 140,
Wellingborough, Northants NN8 4ZA United Kingdom
Email: info@ospreydirect.co.uk

The Marketing Manager, Osprey Direct USA,
c/o Motorbooks International, PO Box 1,
Osceola, WI 54020-0001, USA
Email: info@ospreydirectusa.com

www.ospreypublishing.com

## Acknowledgements

The Introduction and Chapters 3 to 7 were written by Geoff Coughlin.

Chapters 1 is by Julio C. Cabos Gómez. Chapter 2 is by Juan M. Villalba Dominguez, Julio C. Cabos Gómez, Rodrigo Navarro Díaz and Aurelio Gimeno Ruiz.

Colour profiles by Rodrigo Hernández Cabos and Julio C. Cabos Gómez.

Linework by Carlos de Diego Vaquerizo.

# CONTENTS

# INTRODUCTION

## BRIEF HISTORY OF THE SPITFIRE

Unlike its stable-mate the Hawker Hurricane whose airframe underwent comparatively little development throughout its service, the Supermarine Spitfire ended its career well after WWII a very different aircraft from the Mark I that first gained fame when it fought alongside the Hurricane during the Battle of Britain. After this notable beginning, the Spitfire flew in most combat theatres until the end of the war and engaged virtually every type of enemy aircraft.

Designed by R. J. Mitchell, the Spitfire was intended to replace the Bristol Bulldog biplane fighter in RAF service. Vickers' chief test pilot 'Mutt' Summers first flew the prototype on 5 March 1935. The first operational unit to receive the Spitfire was No. 19 Squadron, based at Duxford in 1938. The Spitfire did not go to France in 1939–40 or take part in the early war campaigns in Norway or the Middle East. In fact, at the start of the Battle of Britain, there were far fewer Spitfires in service than Hurricanes. This was mainly due to the longer development time for the Spitfire as well as difficulties in setting up production at the main

BELOW **A terrific plan view of a Spitfire Mk I, seen in 1938. Note the two-blade propeller and large over-wing roundels with broad yellow borders.**

facility at Castle Bromwich. The first Spitfire 'kill' was achieved near the Royal Navy's base in the Firth of Forth on 16 October 1939, when a Heinkel 111 was shot down. The main Spitfire base during the battle of Britain was RAF Hornchurch and its satellite airfield at Rochford where six squadrons were located (Nos. 41, 54, 65, 74, 222 and 603).

Development of the Spitfire went hand in hand with the improvements made to the front-line types of the Luftwaffe such as the Messerschmitt Bf 109 and later the Focke-Wulf 190. Early on the Bf 109E and Mk I and II Spitfires were fairly evenly matched. The Mk V, which entered service in March 1941, was the next major Spitfire version. This had a more powerful engine and appeared in three major sub-types with different wing designs and armament fits. However, the Mk V was quickly found to be outclassed first by the Bf 109F and then the Fw 190 when that design appeared. This caused the next major modification to the Spitfire in the form of the Mk IX. Only with this version did many pilots feel that they had the fighter to challenge the Fw 190 on anything like equal terms. A yet more powerful Merlin engine helped enormously, not to mention some of the other modifications such as the lengthened fuselage, and broad chord rudder that was fitted to some aircraft.

By the spring of 1942, with the threat of an invasion of England receding, thoughts could turn to sending Spitfires to serve overseas at last. Malta was in serious need of an effective defence capability and the Spitfire was clearly the best aircraft available to meet the challenge of the Luftwaffe's fighters head-on. As a result the first Tropicalised version of the Spitfire was born, the Mk V Trop. The aircraft were very clearly distinguishable with their chin-mounted Vokes Multi-Vee dust filter for the carburettor intake. In addition to this version there were some very interesting Spitfire variants like the HF VII that featured a pressure cabin and pointed wingtips for better performance at high altitude. An

ABOVE **A Mk V of No. 133 (Eagle) Squadron, seen on 8 May 1942. Note the three-bladed propeller and 'fish-tail' exhaust outlets.**

ABOVE **A Mk IX of 421 Squadron RAF, as seen in 1943. Just visible are the clipped wingtips and four-bladed prop. Note the unusually high position of the fuselage serial number.**

improved Merlin 61 also helped this capability.

The next substantial improvement to the Spitfire was the replacement of the Rolls-Royce Merlin with the considerably more advanced Griffon engine, the Spitfire Mk XIV prototype in 1941 being the first operational British fighter to be equipped with the Griffon. Including a more powerful engine also made a number of significant structural changes necessary. The first production model of the Spitfire to be fitted with the Griffon, however, was the Mk XII, such as those supplied to No. 41 Squadron. Griffon-engined Spitfires achieved considerable success against Fw 190 'tip-and-run' attacks. The considerable speed of the Mk XIV (450–550mph in a dive) was also put to good use again in the fight against the V-1 flying bomb. Rather than destroy these by gunfire, when the explosion would be dangerous to the fighter, the aircraft often flew alongside the V-1 and brought one wingtip up underneath the wingtip of the V-1. The airflow was disrupted causing the V-1 to spiral out of control – very effective.

Eventually the Spitfire went on to be developed into 24 different Marks and remained in production until 1947.

## MODEL SPITFIRES THEN AND NOW

To the delight of many Supermarine Spitfire modellers, this famous type has enjoyed a resurgence of interest from the main kit manufacturers in recent years. The good news is that the popular scales are very well served today. In recent years both Tamiya and Hasegawa have produced excellent models of the Spitfire Mks I and V in 1/48 'quarter scale'. In the smaller 1/72 scale Tamiya has a Mk I and Fujimi has examples of the later Griffon-powered 'Spits' which are very nicely executed, albeit difficult to get hold of. Airfix has always had a strong reputation for kitting RAF types and the Spitfire is no exception. Who can forget their massive 1/24 scale Mk I – a genuine Superkit dating back 30 years? Crammed with detail, this largely accurate model is still available today. The early pressings of this kit featured white plastic and a number of features that are common on that large-scale series: retractable undercarriage and sliding canopy to mention just two. Isn't it surprising that so few completed 1/24 Spitfires can be seen at model shows around the world?

Airfix caused great waves in the model world when a few years ago the company released examples of the late Mark Spitfire F 22-24 and the Royal Navy Seafire equivalents the FR 46 and 47 in 1/48 scale. The whole quality of these toolings is more akin to that of Tamiya or Hasegawa than those models produced on home soil in the UK. The fit of the parts is generally very good and outline shape excellent.

It is important not to forget Matchbox in this brief round-up of Spitfire modelling over the years. Although difficult to obtain, their 1/32 F 22/24 is a genuinely nice model. Of course it bears some of the less fortunate Matchbox hallmarks such as the deep trenches representing panel lines. However, in a model of this large scale it is a straightforward task to fill these and re-scribe more realistic new ones.

As you go back over the years there have been some interesting variants of the Spitfire. In 1/48 scale, Otaki/ARII produced a Mk VIII that featured the more pointed broad chord rudder. The quality of the tooling is pretty good – the only real failing being the lack of the distinctive 'gull-wing' shape beneath the fuselage. However, if you combine this model, perhaps with the old Airfix Mk V, it is possible to create a Mk IX or even a T Mk IX. In the latter case, however, you will need to install a second cockpit! In a twist of irony, the Otaki Mk VIII is still available under the Airfix label in 1/48 scale. This 'swapping' of moulds is quite common these days and so it is worth checking on the originality of the moulds you are buying. A call to your model shop, supplier or even the manufacturer will usually clarify the position.

Perhaps the greatest disappointment to Spitfire modellers over the years has been the lack of a decent model of the Mk IX in quarter scale, particularly in the light of this type's significance to the RAF. This is perhaps understandable to a point, in that the manufacturers get several of the main variants out of the same Mk I and V tooling. The resin and etched metal after-market manufacturers like Airwaves have helped improve one or two of the latest offerings, notably by Occidental and MPM. As we go to press Hasegawa have finally filled the gap and introduced an excellent Mk IXc in quarter scale. This kit features superb tooling and detailed options such as choice of rudders, wingtips and stores.

If the smaller 1/72 scale is your preferred choice, then some excellent kits are currently available – especially the Mk Vb from Revell. In addition the Griffon Spitfires are also available courtesy of specialist conversions supplied by Brigade Models.

Going back to the 1970s, the older and possibly more experienced modellers may recall the 'Dogfight-Double' series produced by Airfix in 1/72 scale. We remember so well the Mk IX Spitfire overshooting the damaged Messerschmitt Bf 110 and perhaps this era was the one that, through fantastic box art, did so much to promote the hobby.

In conclusion, it is perhaps fitting to end this short ride through history by noticing that the kit makers have largely ignored the Spitfire prototype K5054. Recently though, Neil Burkill, who produces the excellent Paragon range of resin and etched accessories, has remedied this situation – well done Neil!

BELOW **They don't come bigger than this. The Airfix 1/24 Spitfire is now available in Mk I or Mk V versions.**

# MODELLING THE SPITFIRE Mk V

BELOW **The classic lines of the Merlin-engined Spitfire are evident in this photograph.**

The scale modeller really is spoilt for choice when it comes to building a scale replica of the Vickers Supermarine Spitfire. The Mk V is a good option because it is available in all the main scales and from several different manufacturers. The 1/48 scale model from Hasegawa is featured here – and what a nice model kit it is, too. Finely recessed panel lines, excellent fit of parts and accurate as well – it doesn't get much better does it? You do have a choice, though, and could pick a

Mark V from just about any scale, or indeed begin with a kit of the earlier Mark I/II – the choice is yours.

Of course having a wide choice of scale model kits is always desirable, but often the decision to start a particular project will be just as much about the availability and quality of suitable reference material. And there are plenty of references readily available for the Mk V Spitfire. The reference section towards the end of this book identifies some of the texts featuring the Spitfire Mk V plus many other variants that are available in kit form. These include the Mks I and II already mentioned as well as the Mk IX, for so long eagerly awaited, and the Mk XIV.

# SPITFIRE MARK Vb

The renowned Japanese manufacturer Hasegawa has several excellent models of the Spitfire. The first of these, which is featured here, reproduces in 1/48 scale the version of this legendary British fighter plane of which the greatest number of examples were built – the Mk V.

This model, catalogue reference JT4, includes decals for aircraft of three RAF units: No. 303 (Polish) Squadron, No. 401 (Canadian) Squadron, and 2nd (Polish) Fighter Wing. The second option produced by this manufacturer is JT7, a Spitfire Mk VI and they have recently added a long-awaited Mk IX to their quarter-scale range.

The delicacy and quality of the detail in the Mk V kit is quite remarkable on its own, but we have improved upon it with Eduard photo-etched sets 48-103 and 48-107. The first of these sheets is for detailing the interior of the cockpit, and the second is for the

RIGHT **The instrument panel was reconstructed in plastic, because the photo-etched parts do not fit correctly onto the model.**

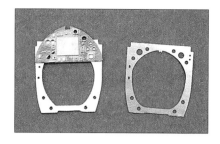

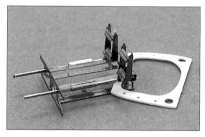

FAR RIGHT **The pedal structure was completed with fine 0.6mm metal tubes.**

FAR RIGHT, BELOW **Part of the floor and one of the structural bulkheads were also made from plastic sheet.**

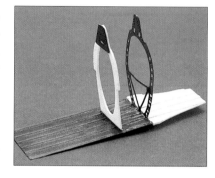

main flaps. In some cases the photo-etched parts do not fit the Hasegawa model precisely so in these examples we used them as patterns for producing our own detail work.

## Cockpit Interior

The cockpit interior is almost entirely composed of Eduard photo-etched parts. We followed the Eduard instructions for the control column, seat, side panels, etc. The difficulties, mentioned above, in fitting some of these correctly, led us to make our own out of plastic strips. These problem parts included the structural reinforcement in the pedal section and the area behind the seat. All the connections, framework and reinforcements for tubular

BOTH RIGHT **The photo-etched seat includes fine tubular parts which make up its structure, made from metal rods and plastic.**

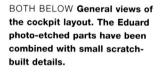

BOTH BELOW **General views of the cockpit layout. The Eduard photo-etched parts have been combined with small scratch-built details.**

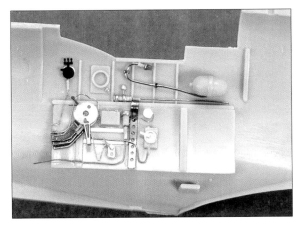
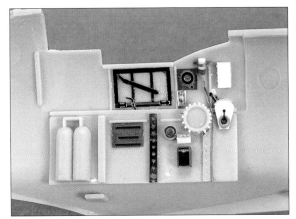
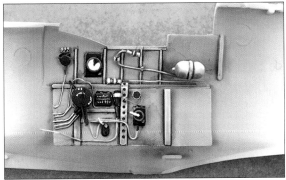

parts were constructed, according to the required width, from copper wire and metal rods produced by Minimeca.

Before continuing with further improvements the two halves of the fuselage had to be joined, and we therefore needed to paint the interior of the cockpit.

We started by painting the whole interior with an airbrush, using Gunze Sangyo acrylic green H312. The next step was to outline and paint the various panels, which we did with oil washes, first with dark earth brown and then with olive green. This was later complemented with dry brush work using medium green 891 mixed with a little blue green 974, in this case from the Vallejo Model Color paint range.

This combination of washes and dry-brush work enables the smallest detail in the cockpit area to be reproduced. For the washes, always use a shade which is darker than the base colour. The oil paint, which should be very diluted, should be applied around the detail and let run into the various nooks and crannies. In contrast, we used dry-brush work to accentuate the relief detail. Here it is best to use one or more tones, lighter than the base colour, with a flat brush applied to the edges and surfaces. After this general work, we moved on to painting

ABOVE, ALL FOUR **Cockpit interior side panels. Much of the detail has been modified, such as the control lever for the undercarriage. The base colour for the cockpit interior is RAF interior grey-green, which we reproduced using Gunze Sangyo green H312. To accentuate the detail we applied oil washes in dark earth brown and olive green.**

LEFT **The final touches to complete the cockpit interior were added by hand, using paints in this instance from the Vallejo range of acrylics.**

ABOVE **The completed No. 303 (Polish) Squadron model. Note the panel line weathering appearing through the decals for a more realistic finish.**

RIGHT **The undercarriage on the Spitfire is very straightforward. Even so, it is necessary to add small details, such as pipes and supports.**

RIGHT **The tail wheel and main landing gear assemblies. Note the ink wash in the recesses to give that realistic effect.**

each small detail, using the usual techniques. The various panels, levers, gunsight, etc. were painted in matt black, the footrest in leather brown, and the seat harness in khaki brown. Finally we painted the pedals in matt aluminium XF16 by Tamiya, and the oxygen hose in white.

Once the cockpit was painted we joined the fuselage halves. At this point the interior of the cockpit has to be protected so that no damage is done and no dust from filing or sanding gets in. Tamiya masking tape is ideal.

## The Wings

Before gluing the wings you will need to cut out sections of the lower wing for the flaps. The flaps can be created using the relevant Eduard photo-etched parts, displaying them in the open position and revealing their internal structure. It is important that the cutting line is very precise, so that the etched parts fit perfectly, particularly the linings in the upper wings. The easiest method is to make a series of successive incisions with a knife point along the cutting lines. Consider using a new blade for this job.

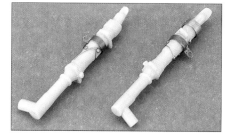

Once the plastic flaps were removed, the edges were filed clean and then the etched parts secured in place. It was necessary to use filler at the joins in the upper flaps. The lower section has an axle which extends from one end of the

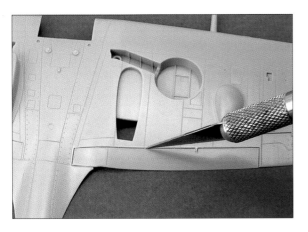

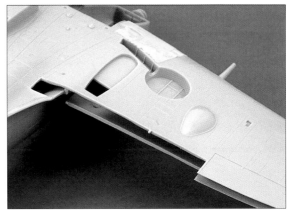

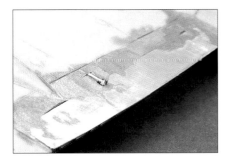

flap to the other, and this was reproduced using a 0.5mm metal rod. The flap opening mechanism also needs to be assembled, on the upper section of the wing, and again it is a photo-etched part.

## Other Details

The detail on the undercarriage is very straightforward. All we did was replace the existing torque links with photo-etched parts and their respective cables. Other improvements were replacing the original barrels for the guns with hollow steel tubes by Minimeca.

## Colour scheme

To finish our Spitfire we opted to use the decals in the kit, choosing the aircraft with the RF*M identification letters and serial number AR335, belonging to No. 303 (Polish) Squadron, RAF. This squadron was the second Polish squadron to be created in Britain and their Spits bore a small national flag and the emblem of the Kosciuszko Squadron.

TOP LEFT **Cutting off the original plastic flaps by making a series of incisions with the point of a very sharp craft knife.**

ABOVE **Next we secured both wings provisionally with a strip of masking tape, to check the accuracy of the cut.**

ABOVE LEFT **The internal structure of the photo-etched flaps includes very fine ribbing which is very tricky to assemble.**

LEFT **The upper flaps need to be filled with putty to fit perfectly against the wing.**

BELOW LEFT **The completed lower flaps in the port wing. The drooped lower section was secured using cyanoacrylate glue.**

BELOW **The lower radiator door is movable and made from a thin piece of scrap plastic sheet.**

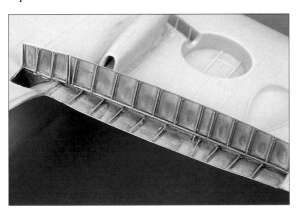

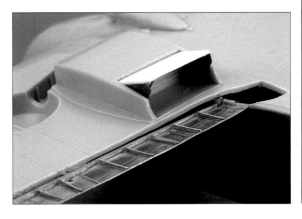

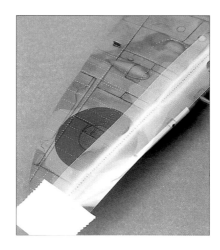

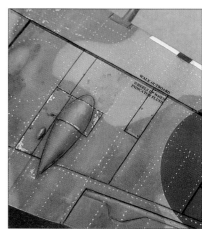

RIGHT **A piece of acetate with minute perforations can be used to paint the rivets. This material is very flexible and adapts to any shape, and can be secured with adhesive tape.**

FAR RIGHT **The chipped paint effect is achieved using a paintbrush and metallic grey.**

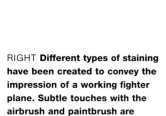

RIGHT **Different types of staining have been created to convey the impression of a working fighter plane. Subtle touches with the airbrush and paintbrush are needed to achieve the effect.**

RIGHT BOTH **In the upper picture you can see the interior colour is sprayed first, showing through when viewed from inside. The fuselage colour is applied next, ensuring continuity with the overall camouflage pattern when viewed from above.**

RIGHT **The small window pane in the main canopy was cut out and replaced with a piece of acetate, stuck with white (PVA) glue.**

This Mk Vb Spitfire has the usual RAF colour scheme from the summer of 1941 onwards, of ocean grey with dark green for the upper surfaces, distributed according to the 'A' scheme, and lower surfaces in medium sea grey. The upper wing surfaces have Type B roundels, 40 inches in diameter, and the lower wing surfaces bear Type A roundels. The propeller spinner and the rear band on the fuselage are in sky.

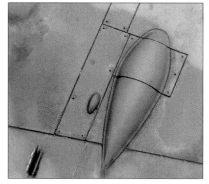

## Paintwork

We began by airbrushing all lower surfaces with medium sea grey, choosing Gunze Sangyo H306 grey as it is a fairly close equivalent. We then continued to work on the lower surfaces, producing effects of damage, wear and tear by combining fine airbrushed lines with oil washes applied by brush, to highlight the structural lines. The interior of the undercarriage well was painted Gunze Sangyo H332 light aircraft grey.

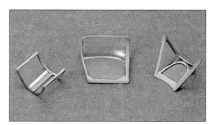

We then painted all the upper surfaces in the lighter ocean grey shade, which we obtained by mixing Tamiya medium blue XF18, sky XF21 and dark grey XF24. This mixture then needs to be lightened, with sky grey XF19 and sprayed very gently to create a somewhat muted effect.

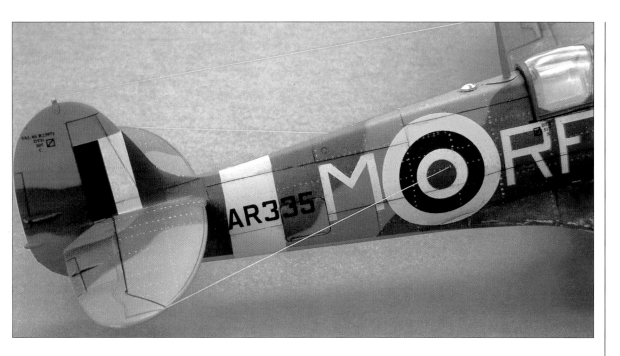

The exact equivalent for the dark green second colour on the upper surfaces is Gunze Sangyo H309. You now need to mask the green before spraying the ocean grey. You can use paper cut to shape or thin rolls of Blu-Tac putty to create the edge you want, but keep the rolls thin to simulate a near-hard edge. The paper stencil will produce soft edges, if the distance between the paper and the surfaces is adjusted while airbrushing, but it is important to keep the nozzle of the airbrush as perpendicular as possible to the edges of the paper, otherwise paint can seep underneath. However, note that RAF aircraft mainly had a hard edge demarcation between the colours, so don't lift the paper masks too far from the surface.

Once the complete colour scheme has been reproduced, we can then move on to the insignia and other markings. The lettering and

ABOVE **The cables for the antennae were made from strips of plastic. You can use very fine fishing line or stretched sprue to good effect too.**

LEFT **Although they look large, the size of the Spitfire decals is correct for the period depicted. The whole model should be given a coat of gloss varnish if you are using acrylics or matt enamel. This will help to hide the decal carrier film when the final coat of varnish is applied.**

**15**

identifying band on the fuselage were painted in duck egg green H74. For the rest of the insignia, like the maple leaf badge and the tricolour band on the tail, we used the decals from the kit.

We now need to create the various effects of wear and tear, particularly on the wings and some areas of the fuselage. To achieve this we used a combination of airbrush and paint brush effects. It is very important to study historical photographs of the Spitfire in order to recreate these effects with

**This overall view of the fighter plane shows the widespread wear and tear effects on the lower surfaces. The grey base colour is an ideal backdrop for a wide range of colours.**

accuracy. We applied lighter staining in areas, using an airbrush.

On the dark green sections we used a mixture of Gunze Sangyo green H308 and H74. We used various green and blue-green acrylic tones, applied by brush.

LEFT **When applying the small decals, first apply a coat of gloss varnish to the designated area, or preferably the whole surface, to avoid any tonal variations created by the varnish.**

Contrasts were created in some areas by shading with oils, mixing dark ultramarine blue and dark earth brown. Next, to create shading and reproduce various effects of wear and tear, we combined fine airbrushed lines and selected oil washes, applied with

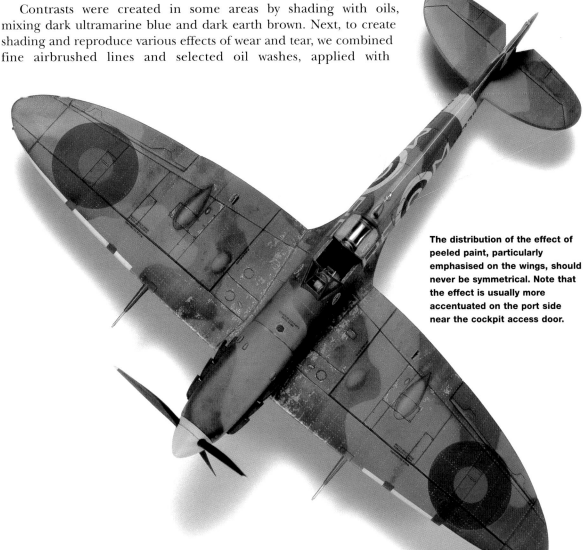

**The distribution of the effect of peeled paint, particularly emphasised on the wings, should never be symmetrical. Note that the effect is usually more accentuated on the port side near the cockpit access door.**

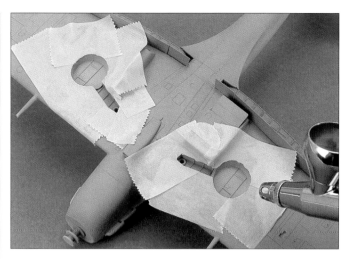

a brush. A small piece of paper can be used as a stencil to create tiny stains in specific areas with the airbrush.

The exhausts were painted with acrylics. The base colour is brown, which we then lightened with dark blue-grey to achieve the effect of burnt metal.

Stencil decals are applied all over the plane to indicate the location of various controls and panels. These can be added once the designated area has been given a coat of gloss varnish. Some of these decals require the use of Micro Set and Micro Sol liquids to help them bed down over surface detail. Once these are in place, a further coat of satin varnish can be applied. This will take away any sign of the decal carrier film.

ABOVE **After applying the base colour to the lower surfaces, protect with masking tape when you paint the hatches for the landing gear.**

The final touches, before assembling the antennae and the cockpit canopy, consisted of creating a peeled paint effect on the wings and the fuselage. For this we used metallic grey XF56 in Tamiya enamel. Various other shades of grey can also be used to good effect.

RIGHT & BELOW RIGHT **Note the highlights to the lower wing applied with an airbrush. The wash used to weather the recesses can be clearly seen. Note, too, the fully drooped position of the flap.**

BELOW **Perforated acetate secured with masking tape is used with the airbrush to complete the rivet detailing around the cockpit.**

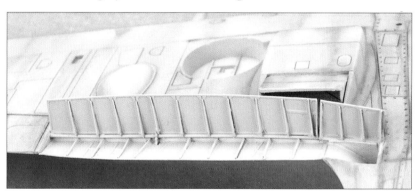

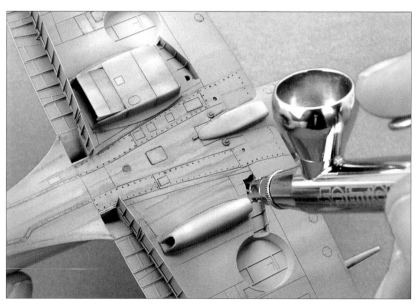

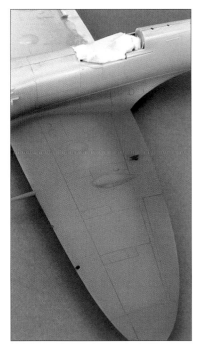

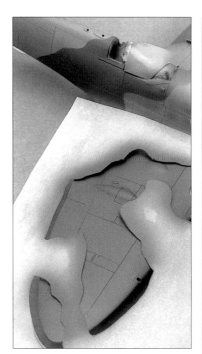
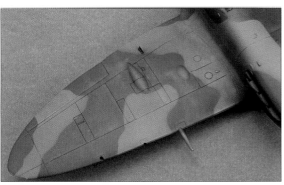
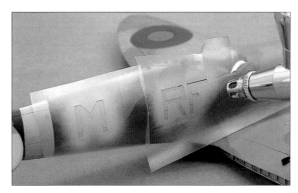
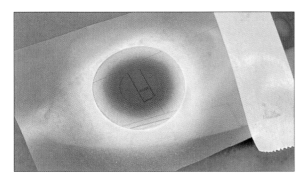
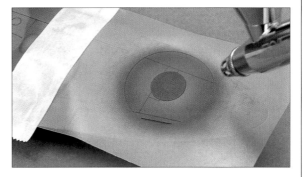

TOP ROW, LEFT **We began work on the upper surfaces by applying the basic ocean grey camouflage colour.**

TOP ROW, CENTRE **Using the same grey colour, but in a somewhat lighter tone, we gave a slight highlight to the paintwork.**

TOP ROW, RIGHT **Next we masked out the camouflage and applied dark green, using a piece of paper as a stencil.**

MIDDLE ROW, LEFT **We then created the same highlight effect on the dark green.**

MIDDLE ROW, RIGHT **Although the procedure is laborious, a more realistic finish can be achieved if the the lettering and fuselage band are painted on.**

BOTTOM ROW, BOTH **We used the same method for the roundels. Accurate masking is essential.**

# SPITFIRE Mk Vb TROP

ABOVE **The Spitfire Mk Vb Trop in distinctive Mediterranean markings. The weathering is noteworthy around the engine cowl and spinner.**

It seems that the Spitfire is once again a popular subject among the model manufacturers. Different versions of this classic fighter, reproduced in all scales, have been brought onto the market recently.

It is a strange that the three big Japanese model producers should all have brought out a variety of kits of the legendary Spitfire at much the same time. Fujimi and Tamiya opted for the 1/72 scale, Tamiya, again, and Hasegawa have chosen 1/48 scale. Monogram produced a 1/48 Spitfire kit in the past and if you search around you can still find examples. This is a good option if you are on a tight budget. It is up to the modeller to select his/her preferred model, according to personal tastes and requirements.

Hasegawa have opted to reproduce two Mk Vb Spitfires, a Mk VI, now a Mk IX, and the one covered by this article, the Spitfire Mk Vb Trop (kit ref. JT-5). This version featured a Vokes sand-filter system which enabled the aircraft to operate successfully around the Mediterranean region and North Africa. This kit includes transfers for you to produce three RAF examples and one for the Turkish Air Force. Our model bears the insignia and numbering of No. 145 Squadron RAF.

The kit is generally quite accurate, although yet further detail may be added using the Eduard set of photo-etched parts ref. 48/103 which provides a complete cockpit interior, in addition to various items connected with the cockpit canopy, undercarriage and radiators.

OPPOSITE **The completed No. 303 Squadron Mk V model.**

ABOVE **The top surfaces are primed with the lighter of the two colours that make up the camouflage.**

ABOVE RIGHT **The colour for the under-surfaces is equivalent to FS-3523 azure blue.**

RIGHT **Once the model has been varnished and the decals put in place, the panel lines are enhanced.**

BELOW **Cockpit interior of a Spitfire Mk II. This gives a good impression of the overall cockpit layout.**

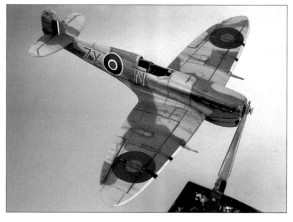

## Assembly

The kit assembly work is generally pretty simple, since the clean moulding of the parts means they fit together quite well. The cabin interior in the kit parts and mouldings is very detailed although it can be enhanced if we put in the Eduard etched metal seat together with the appropriate extras on the fret.

The instrument panel also benefits substantially by using the etched metal accessories, although we made use of the supporting bracket included with the model (part C3), cutting it across near the bottom and then mounting the various photo-etched parts on it. We followed the usual processes to glue on the remainder of the items that make up the model. It is a good idea to use a glue that acts on the joins in a capillary manner, with filler being applied on top of the joins subsequently, taking very great care not to spoil the lines of the panels that will later be marked onto these areas too much. Using a fine abrasive we then carefully rubbed over all the leading edges and projections of the canopy as well as the curves of the air intake, rendering them as smooth as possible.

The version we chose necessitates the assembly of the De Havilland propeller (parts B3, B5 and B6) and the ventral launcher system and bomb.

## Painting

Our model is finished in the RAF tropical camouflage scheme, comprising sky azure blue under surfaces, and upper surfaces of dark earth and mid stone. To reproduce this scheme we used an airbrush and Gunze Sangyo paints, using standard paper stencils to separate the colours.

We made the blue shade for the lower surfaces by mixing 85% Gunze Sangyo bluish grey H42, with 5% light grey H61

**ABOVE & ABOVE LEFT The interior of the model is very complete but can be improved still further using various items in the etched metal set.**

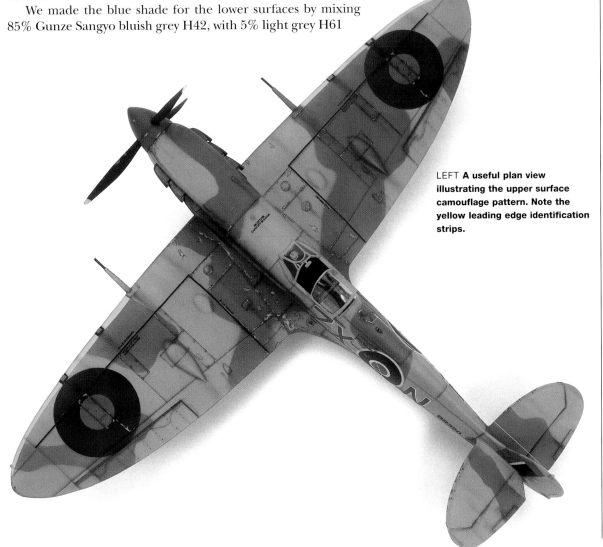

**LEFT A useful plan view illustrating the upper surface camouflage pattern. Note the yellow leading edge identification strips.**

RIGHT **The Mk Vb Trop was used for bombing raids, too, as can be seen here. Note the Vokes dust filter under the chin.**

RIGHT **Slight effects of wear and tear and chipped paint are also reproduced on the roundel decals.**

FAR RIGHT **Detail on the bomb rack and bomb, finished off with varying degrees of shine.**

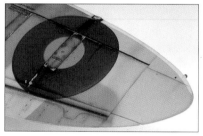

and 10% dark navy grey H75. Alternatively it may be easier to use a tin of azure blue from one of the mainstream paint ranges, such as Xtracolor, Poly 5, or Humbrol. For the lighter brown (mid stone) shade of the camouflage we used Gunze Sangyo H71 while the dark earth colour is H72.

The cockpit interior was given a green H212 primer coat to represent RAF interior grey green, after which the minor detail was added by brush. The propeller spinner is in H3 red and the propeller blades are in H12 matt black with their tips in H4 yellow.

RIGHT **The yellow strip on the leading edge of the wings was painted with the assistance of adhesive masking.**

FAR RIGHT **The narrow chord of the undercarriage can be seen here.**

RIGHT **We reproduced small signs of paint chipping in the wing recesses with a fine brush and aluminium colour.**

FAR RIGHT **To define the camouflage edges we used standard paper stencils cut using a blade.**

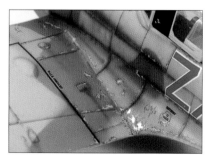

After we applied the basic colours from our scheme we proceeded to reproduce some effects of wear and tear, again using the airbrush. A mixture of Holbein sepia and grey tones was used to define the lines of the panels, these colours fitting in very well with the brown shades of the camouflage. A good alternative shade also

ABOVE **A very good front three-quarter view of the completed model showing all the identifying features of the 'Trop' version.**

LEFT **The effects of wear and tear on the lower sections of the model are a little more noticeable.**

worth trying is Tamiya X19 smoke. The same method is used again to apply light watercolour shades to certain breaks in detail such as rivets and the engine cowling latches. The exhaust staining naturally has to be

LEFT **We also produced small signs of chipped paint on the leading edges of the wings.**

FAR LEFT **The exhaust stains aft of the outlet pipes were sprayed with an airbrush, work undertaken with the paint well thinned.**

## COLOUR CHART

**Camouflage scheme**
*Top surfaces:* medium brown H71, dark earth H72
*Bottom surfaces:* 85% H42, 5% H61, 1-% H75

**Detail**
*Interiors:* green H212
*Propeller spinner :* red H3
*Propeller blades:* matt black H12
*Bomb bracket:* grey H306
*Bomb:* dark green H309
*All Gunze Sangyo colours*

ABOVE RIGHT **The antennae cables are very fine filaments of stretched plastic, glued on with small amounts of cyanoacrylate.**

BELOW **Note here how the roundels stand out, being neatly sprayed on.**

done in a darker shade, as has that of the guns and ventral streamlining vents. For these areas we used a selection of brown tones heavily darkened with black.

It is important to use the adhesive paper correctly in order to carry out the masking properly, something that requires great precision, as does protecting the transparent parts of the cabin and painting the yellow strip on the leading edge of the wings. It is a good idea to cut the masking out over a drawing that matches the curvature and size of the parts.

26

# MODELLING OTHER SPITFIRE VARIANTS

This chapter will describe three different versions of this classic World War II fighter whose stylish silhouette and unmistakable wing shape make it indispensable to the collection of any model aircraft enthusiast. We begin with the Mk I, which gained fame during the Battle of Britain, continue with a Mk IX, as flown in 1944 by Johnnie Johnson, the top-scoring British ace of the war, and conclude with the Griffon-engined PR XIX.

## SPITFIRE Mk I

Various kits were available to produce our Mk I. We chose the Tamiya example in 1/48, since its details are in general highly accurate. However, we should point out that careful measurement will show that this representation is in fact some 1.5mm short of the correct scale length. We would recommend getting hold of as many references as possible, most importantly the excellent *Aero Detail No. 8*.

LEFT **The Aero Detail books are simply stunning, with plenty of detailed colour photographs and profiles/drawings of the real aircraft.**

BELOW **The Tamiya Mk I kit in 1/48 is a joy to build and made the choice of kit easy.**

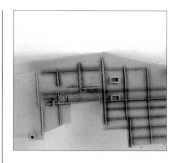

ABOVE **You paint the fuselage interior sections in British Grey Green.**

ABOVE RIGHT **With the help of a sharp blade we separate the door from the fuselage.**

RIGHT **As they are very delicate, the cockpit parts are assembled after the dry-brush process.**

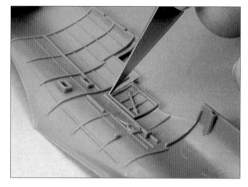

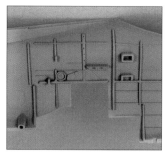

ABOVE **Once the paint is dry we shade with an airbrush.**

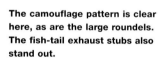

The camouflage pattern is clear here, as are the large roundels. The fish-tail exhaust stubs also stand out.

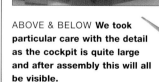

ABOVE & BELOW **We took particular care with the detail as the cockpit is quite large and after assembly this will all be visible.**

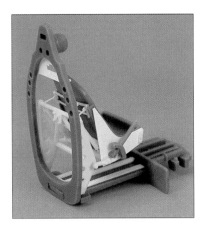
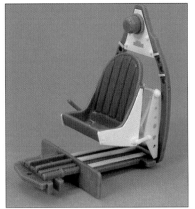

## Assembly

The sides of the cabin are extremely well detailed in the kit mouldings. We started by cleaning off the mould ejectors' stamps and separating the door with a craft knife, then proceeded to paint the interior in British Grey Green which we chose to mix from the following Tamiya colours: XF65 20%, XF21 70% and XF5 10%. Some modellers will prefer to use a ready-mixed paint from another manufacturer. Afterwards we shaded this section with an airbrush and added highlights with a smooth dry brush, lightening the base colour. All details were added later.

We next got the seat and cockpit floor ready, opting to discard the seat support, which is not up to the standard of the rest of the kit. We rebuilt the entire structure and added belts made from fine tin sheet.

ABOVE, ALL THREE **The original seat assembly is very crude and lacking in detail, so we rebuilt it. Once complete it looks much more realistic but you have to take care as the final structure is very delicate.**

LEFT **You should handle the structures you have made with great care, shading with an airbrush and gently bringing out the highlights with a dry brush.**

BELOW **Opening the pilot's access door makes a real difference. The classic lines of R. J. Mitchell's design speak for themselves.**

RIGHT **The detail on the control panel is excellent, simply requiring the addition of a few minor items.**

The front panel of the cockpit is excellent and you simply need to finish it off with minor details such as plating and an electrical switch located on the lower section.

One of the strong points of the Tamiya model is the assembly, which can be described as exquisite, as the components fit together with such precision that it is completely unnecessary to use filler.

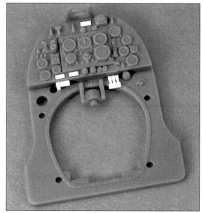

## Painting

Having completed the assembly phase we started to paint the model. We used Tamiya acrylics but would not recommend that

RIGHT **The wing sections are joined using liquid glue.**

FAR RIGHT **The kit cockpit offers an excellent level of detail.**

BELOW **The completed Tamiya Mk I Spitfire. Note the night coloured undersurface of the port wing and high visibility roundel.**

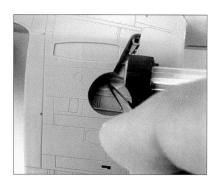

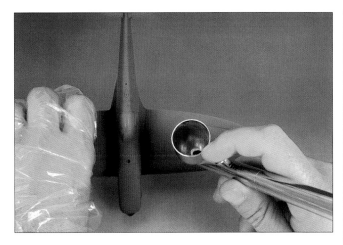

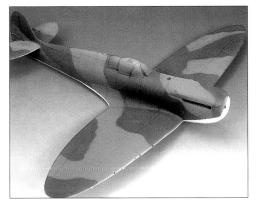

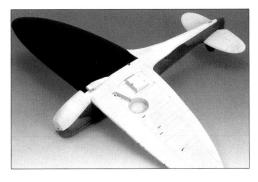

you follow the mixtures which are given by the manufacturer, as the colours produced are entirely inappropriate. The correct mixtures are as follows:

ABOVE LEFT **It is helpful to use a reference chart to check the original colours.**

ABOVE **The upper section is first covered with the lighter colour, in this case dark earth**

BOTH LEFT **Once the painting process is complete the plane is ready to be gloss varnished prior to applying the decals.**

### Upper surfaces

**Dark Earth:** 70% XF52 + 25% XF62 + 5% XF58

**Dark Green:** 40% XF65 + 40% XF62 + 20% XF-11.

### Lower surfaces

**Sky (Duck egg blue):** 90% XF21 + 10% XF2

**Black:** 100% XF1

Alternatively an easier option might be to use RAF Dark Earth and Dark Green from one of the mainstream paint manufacturers, as previously described.

The colour scheme selected is that used on patrols over the Channel and incursions over the French coast after the Battle of Britain, which includes a combination of sky blue and black on the lower surfaces. We airbrushed the lower section in the two colours and then protected it with an adhesive mask to avoid it being stained by the colours from the upper section.

On the upper section we started by applying the brown colour and, once it was dry, added the RAF Dark Green. It is useful usually to apply the lighter camouflage colour first, as this is easier to cover properly when applying the darker second colour later. Once both colours of paint were dry we applied a coat of gloss varnish, ready for decal application.

The material used in the sheet of decals supplied with the kit is extremely hard, which means that you need to use Micro Set to attach

TOP LEFT **The duck egg strip and the QJ*B code were sprayed on after masking.**

TOP RIGHT **For the green camouflage pattern we used a mask.**

ABOVE **All the antennae cables were made of stretched plastic. Very fine fishing line can also work well.**

ABOVE RIGHT **To reproduce the staining around the exhaust we opted for a very dark shade of brown, rather than black.**

RIGHT **Various small items were painted separately and assembled at the end.**

them and Micro Sol to adapt them. The manufacturer supplies some white circles for use under the roundels, their purpose being to avoid the camouflage pattern showing through. This is fine in theory but in practice the circles are too big and stick out beneath the roundels. This arrangement also makes the combination too thick, so we left these out.

Small parts such as the propeller, undercarriage and radiators should all be assembled and painted separately. We would strongly recommend that you check carefully that they fit on correctly before finishing them: we had to rectify all their attachments.

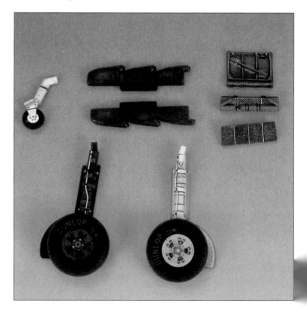

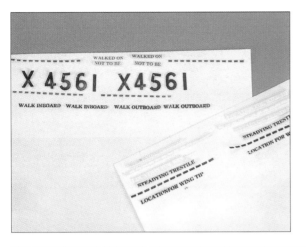

A fret of cockpit canopy parts covering several versions of the fighter is supplied with the kit.

## Final details

We added the most delicate details at the end of the process so as to avoid them being damaged. We started by making the formation lights.

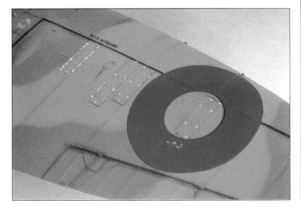

RIGHT **Detail of the completed antennae installation.**

BELOW RIGHT **An underwing shot giving a good impression of the contrasting port and starboard colours.**

The moulded lenses were painted silver, then red, orange and green clear colours were added. Lens covers can then simply be made by scratch-building the parts using pieces of clear acetate sheet. Finally add the antennae using strips of stretched sprue or fishing line.

BELOW **The black area on the wing was worked on using shades of grey, which can also be given a slight bluish tinge.**

BELOW RIGHT **Note the black walk-way lines on the upper wing.**

BOTTOM **The completed model showing off the graceful lines of the Spitfire Mk I.**

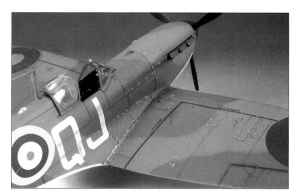

# SPITFIRE LF IXc

ABOVE **The completed Mk IX conversion made from the Tamiya Mk V kit mated to the Hi-Tech and Eduard accessories.**

**W**hen the Focke-Wulf 190 appeared in the skies over France in 1941 it was immediately apparent that it was greatly superior to the Spitfire Mark V, the principal RAF fighter of the time. Fortunately for the RAF, that turn of events coincided almost perfectly with the development of the new Merlin 61 1,565hp engine. Supermarine technicians started preparations to fix this engine in the airframe of the Mk Vb. After various trials, modifications and improvements, carried out in record time, the new Mk IX version was able to go operational in July 1942, going down in history as one of the most important and successful among the many variants of the immortal British fighter. When compared with the Mk V the principal external differences distinguishing the Mk IX were a longer nose, six exhaust pipes on each side, a four-bladed propeller, symmetrical under-wing radiators and a new armament fit.

We built the model using Tamiya's 1/48 Mk V, the best version available on the market. We also used Hi-Tech's resin conversion set and the Eduard photo-engraving set 48-103. Now, of course, you can buy the outstanding new Spitfire Mk IX kit from Hasegawa.

With the nose of the plane cut off, we constructed the interior, using the standard parts that come with the kit on the cockpit sides and the instrument panel, which are excellent and better than any photo-etched alternative. The gunsight was scratch-built. Next we added all the controls (throttle, control wires under the seat and control column) which we completely rebuilt, except for the pedals, which are photo-

RIGHT **The most complicated phase of construction was the need to re-engrave panel lines in the correct positions for the LF IX configuration.**

etched. The pilot's harness was made of tin and copper wire. We also built the seat bracket. The colour used for the interior is Humbrol 78 green, to which we added several washes in burnt umber and a dry-brush coat with the base colour lightened with insignia yellow and white.

Once the fuselage was closed we attached the resin nose and covered the join between the parts with cyanoacrylate. Then we sanded the area down with wet and dry paper and re-engraved the join lines with an engraving tool.

The principal difficulty in the whole project lies in the distribution of panels and weapons fit on the wings, as these differ substantially from those of the Mk V. We used the plans that appear in Squadron Signal 39 *Spitfire*, as a guide. We cut off the entire area to which the new distribution applies and replaced it with plastic card and the new resin cannons and access panels. Once these were glued on we covered the joins with cyanoacrylate and smoothed the surface with sandpaper to enable us then to engrave the new panels, dampers and rivets with an engraving tool like the Olfa P-cutter, for example.

We got rid of the under-wing resin radiators supplied in the Hi-Tech set and kept the one that comes with the Tamiya kit. The one on the starboard wing was obtained from another Tamiya Spitfire. To attach it we pared down the plastic of the wing with a flat blade until the radiator (already having had detail added in the form of wire mesh, acetate or copper wire) fitted on. We used cyano-acrylate to get rid of any grooves that remained once the radiator had been glued on, then evened it out with sandpaper and repaired any panel lines. When you glue the wing onto the

## COLOUR REFERENCE

**INTERIOR**

| | |
|---|---|
| Base colour | Humbrol No. 78 cockpit green |
| Shading | Model Color Vallejo burnt umber |
| Highlights | Base + Humbrol No. 154 (insignia yellow) + Humbrol No. 34 (white) |

**LOWER SURFACES**

| | |
|---|---|
| Medium Sea Grey | Humbrol No. 165 |

**UPPER SURFACES**

| | |
|---|---|
| Dark Green | Humbrol No. 116 |
| Ocean Grey | Humbrol No. 106 |

fuselage you add the carburettor intake beneath the nose and end the assembly phase by attaching the guns, which are resin copies of those that come with the Mk XIV Academy kit. The propeller and undercarriage were assembled and painted separately, with piping made of copper wire.

## Painting and finishing

The aircraft we chose to depict is a Spitfire LF IXc belonging to 144 Wing, based at Ford in June 1944 and piloted by J. E. 'Johnnie' Johnson, the leading RAF fighter ace.

First we applied the white for the 'invasion stripes' (enamel from Revell), which we left masked. We then painted on the grey underside colour and left it to dry, then masked off the upper part with Tamiya masking tape and painted it all over with ocean grey. We left this to dry for a day and then applied the dark green, using masks to obtain very slightly blurred edges. We had to remember to apply the dark green with an airbrush held at a slight angle to the surface so that the air did not lift up our masking templates.

ABOVE **Some structural lines and panels were marked out using selected oil washes.**

Once the camouflage had been painted on, we peeled off the masking tape for the insignia and painted on the roundels, tail pennant and type 'S' sky blue colour band on the fuselage. After this we painted on the black of the invasion stripes and the codes, also in sky blue, together with the propeller spinner. The leading edges of the wings were then painted in Humbrol insignia yellow. Once this painting was completely dry, we applied a coat of Micro gloss varnish. The varnish used at this stage must be an acrylic type given that we shall now go on to use essence of turpentine and oil paints to mark out the panels again, using burnt sienna earth for the upper sections and natural sienna for the lower surfaces and the area of the invasion stripes.

We then proceeded to put on the decals, using only those for the serial number and the Canadian emblem below the cockpit. The decals we used are from the AeroMaster 'Spitfire at war' sheet. We shaded the panels with sepia airbrushing ink from Holbein. To complete the paint scheme we applied a weathered effect to the exhaust stubs and cannon barrels using pastel colours. We fixed the pastels in place with the final varnishing of the model, using a mixture of Revell matt varnish and enamel gloss in a proportion of 9 to 1. You can vary this proportion according to taste so as to increase the level of gloss finish.

We painted the exhaust pipes using a steel primer from Metal Cote (Humbrol) and once this was dry we worked on top of it using matt brown into which we had blended small amounts of orange brown. Finally we completed the model by gluing on the propeller, undercarriage, exhaust pipes and antenna cable, which was made from very fine nylon fishing line.

LEFT **Results of paint chipping at the wing root. The hinged door allows a better view of the work on the detail carried out in the Spitfire's small cockpit.**

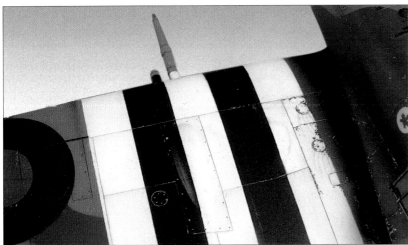

LEFT **The panel lines stand out well against the white identification bands. Weathering the latter carefully is very important if a realistic effect is to be achieved.**

BELOW **The four-blade prop and cannon armament single the Mk IX out as a purposeful war machine.**

# SPITFIRE PR XIX

There are several metal kits on the market for World War II aircraft including one in 1/48 scale by the Italian manufacturer Casadio for the PR XIX photographic reconnaissance version of the Spitfire. In addition to this interesting model, the Casadio catalogue includes the Spitfire series that carried the Griffon 65 engine, such as the Mk XIV, Mk 21 and Seafire Mk 45, together with several versions of the Focke-Wulf 190, among which the Fw 190A5/U15, a torpedo version of the craft not sold by any other firm in this scale, stands out.

## History

The PR XIX was the last Spitfire to have the elliptical wing and, as with all previous photographic reconnaissance craft, it was unarmed. The weapons were replaced with larger fuel tanks (302 litres in this case) located in the leading edges of the wings; the pilot was supplied with a greater quantity of oxygen and the engine had a larger oil reservoir that allowed the aircraft to fly long distance missions,

RIGHT **The overall camouflage colour of PRU blue and fuselage identification bands make for a striking model project.**

BELOW **We used Waldron and Airwaves accessory sets to improve the detail of the model, particularly the interior.**

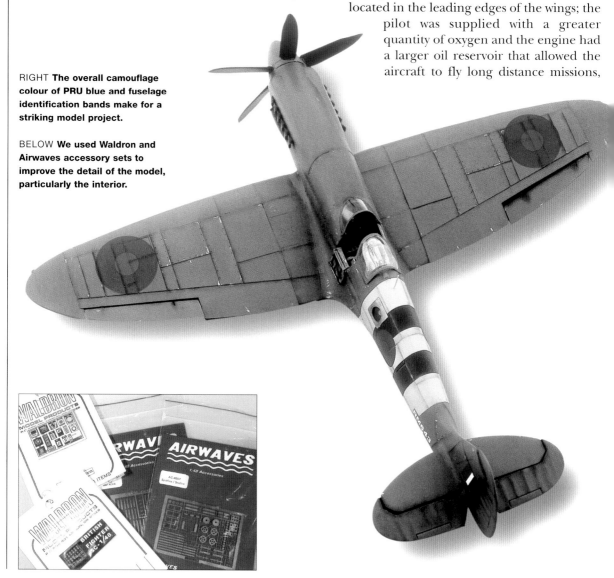

even as far as Berlin itself. The sliding canopy was clear with no framing nor, consequently, bulletproof panels, which provided the pilot with outstanding visibility.

The PR XIX had three cameras, two of which were positioned pointing downwards from the rear fuselage with the third on the port side of the aircraft. The cabin was pressurised. This type was the last RAF Spitfire to remain in service (1954 in Malaysia). A total of 225 of this mark was produced and, while it certainly was not the most numerous of the PR series (471 PR XI craft were built), it had a greater length (91 cm longer than earlier PRs), a five-bladed propeller and longitudinal blisters over the Griffon engine. The particular aircraft we are writing about here is RM643 Z from No. 541 Squadron, based at Benson at the end of 1944, with D-Day stripes on the fuselage only. We found a reference photograph of this aircraft in the Aircam Aviation Series No. 8.

## The Model

The assembly manual contains 40 pages, with a great profusion of drawings and directions. Multi-lingual instructions giving detailed explanations for each of the sequence of steps to be followed during the assembly process are included. The kit contains more than 150 parts, a fair proportion of them photo-etched, together with screws of various types and sizes that are very useful in the assembly of these.

To stick the different parts together we used three types of adhesive: cyano-acrylate liquid and gel and bi-component epoxy glue (5 minutes drying time). The first was used for small parts and the reinforcement of joins, the second for larger parts and those for which a greater margin for manoeuvre was required, and the bi-component adhesive for parts that required maximum resistance and where the weight or shape of the parts rendered this advisable. As regards filler, the ideal solution is to use epoxy putty designed for car bodywork, which is more resistant than that used for plastic.

As far as tools are concerned, in addition to files of various shapes and sizes, it is essential that you have a 2mm screwdriver, given that the larger parts and certain mechanisms fit together with screws, as do the joints of the fuselage, wings, undercarriage etc. To finish off you will also need a pair of flat

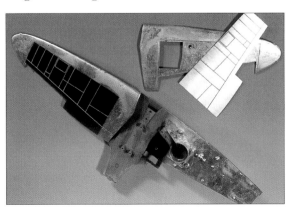

ABOVE, BOTH **The Griffon engine supplied with the model is of excellent quality and its inclusion is optional. To complete the cabling we used copper wire of different thicknesses.**

BELOW **The Griffon-engined Spit was very different from the Merlin-powered versions. Note the bigger fin/rudder, the shape of the upper fuselage aft of the cockpit, and those five propeller blades.**

pliers of the sort used in electronics. Together with the standard tools used for normal plastic modelling work, these complete the set you require.

## Engine

The engine can be included within the kit or alternatively you can display it on a stand. We opted to leave it outside the aircraft because of the excessive thickness of the 'walls' of the kit fuselage, the difficulty of fitting the parts together and the problems brought about by the slightly inaccurate fittings supplied to make the 'working' engine cowling. This decision also allows us to view the whole engine in detail. It has 17 parts, plus 2 separate screws that render the use of adhesive superfluous. Nonetheless, we filled all the joints with liquid cyano-acrylate to strengthen them. We eliminated the attachment brackets for the engine so as to allow us to add the full range of detail work to it. The wiring of the plugs is shown on three photo-etched parts that we stuck onto the distributor, from where they lead off to the sides to meet the relevant plugs. To complete the engine wiring we used 0.1, 0.2 and 0.3mm copper wire, basing our work on the photographs and drawings in Model Art No. 387 *Supermarine Spitfire* which shows the development of all the Spitfire engines. The latest Aero Detail book focuses on the Griffon-engined Spitfire and is also highly recommended.

The engine was painted with metallic black from Model Master. Once the airbrushing was complete, we left it to dry for about 15 or 20 minutes and then polished it with a smooth cloth to obtain the shine that we

required. The wiring should be then painted in metallic grey. Once the engine is fully dry, you apply a very light wash in black acrylic, finishing it off with a dry aluminium brush and highlighting screws and more prominent areas. We made the stand from tiny strips of balsa wood, giving it the height necessary to display the engine block well.

## Interior

All the parts are photo-etched. We added a few improvements such as dials from Waldron (Ref. 4802 –

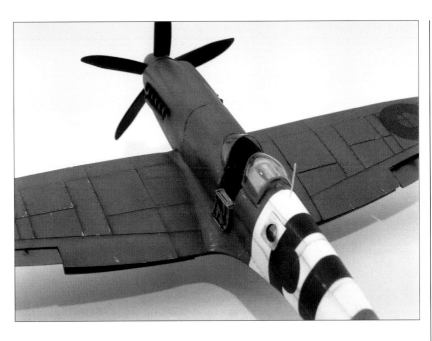

ABOVE **To mark out the panel lines we used black drawing ink. You can also use various shades of brown instead for a slightly more subtle effect.**

British Aircraft Instruments) for the instrument panel and various panels and placards from the same supplier that we can use on the sides (48015 – Spitfire Cockpit Placards & Metal Parts). We also used some Airwaves photo-etched parts. The cockpit sides come moulded on both halves of the fuselage and, although slightly over the top, they do offer a good general impression when supplemented with components from the Waldron set.

The photo-etched parts included in the kit are in a sort of fold-out arrangement containing the various items for each individual part. On the instrument panel section we removed the gunsight since this unarmed PR version did not have one. A headrest for the pilot has to be added onto the protective support and, as the one provided with the model is too small, we replaced this with one made from a round piece of Evergreen plastic. The seat is more complex. The seat itself, its base, and the rudder pedals and other fittings are all included in one opened-out arrangement that has to be gradually folded over bit by bit until you manage to give it the shape required. The belts we used are from Airwaves.

The next step is the assembly of the parts for the camera compartment, to which the main camera, which constitutes a separate item, has then to be added. The gap for the panel through which the photographs were taken, has markings inside so that it can be opened up using an electric drill and then filed to the correct size and shape. We also drilled through the lower part of the fuselage so as to add on the two further cameras included in the PR XIX, as shown in the accompanying drawings.

The tail wheel has to be attached prior to joining the fuselage together, but the one provided with the kit is rather weak and poorly shaped so we discarded it. In its place we used the one from the Arii model (which includes two tail-wheel assemblies) which is more suitable in terms of shape and durability. The interior was painted in RAF grey green. One option is Humbrol 78, matt cockpit green. The instrument

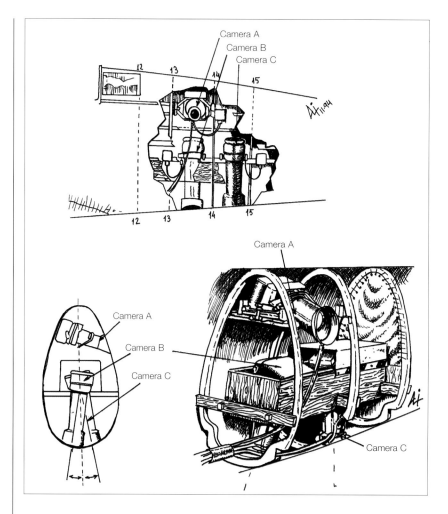

Camera A
Camera B
Camera C

Camera A

Camera A
Camera B
Camera C

Camera C

ABOVE **Diagram of the camera installation.**

panel is black, as are the side panels and upper part of the control column. The camera compartment is also in grey green, while the cameras themselves are black, with a drop of Kristal Klear being added onto the front of the object lenses to produce their characteristic convex shape.

## Fuselage

The joining up of the two parts of the fuselage is one of the most crucial operations of the assembly process. It is a good idea first to attach all the items for the interior on the starboard side, making use of the pegs provided to this end. You have to remember that, as these items are made of metal, any error in assembling them may make it more difficult to fit the two parts of the fuselage together. For this stage we used cyanoacrylate gel, also screwing in the three screws that run along the fuselage to help achieve an extremely solid and accurate attachment. Once they were screwed in, we put covers in place to hide the screws and reinforced the whole fuselage longitudinally with liquid cyanoacrylate.

## Wings

Before attaching the wings, the whole undercarriage system, which is provided in foldout form and with independent suspension, has to be assembled. We rejected the option of folding up the landing gear because this would mean that the model would necessarily have to be handled after it was painted, which would tend to spoil the finish. We simply attached a suspension mechanism to each of its landing struts. The landing gear must be put in place before each part of the wing is attached. We chose to attach it with bi-component glue, which offers greater strength. Each landing gear strut comprises 13 items, including a small main spring that facilitates the operation of the suspension system.

The next step involves putting the flaps and the wing structure in place, this being visible if we leave the flaps down. The pieces are photo-etched and each line of the wing structure has to be put in position. The radiators are also put in place inside the wing, the grilles being made from photo-etched material. Before gluing on the two wing parts, it is a good idea to put a sheet of plastic card in the well in the bottom section of the undercarriage as otherwise it is too deep. Once all the steps indicated have been followed, we proceeded to glue the upper section of each wing onto the lower parts. To do this we used cyanoacrylate gel, as well as screwing in the screws that are provided for each part of the wing. You need to reinforce the wing joint with liquid cyanoacrylate, which you apply along the whole of the leading edge. Then you sand down the locations relating to the weapons because the PR XIX did not carry any.

Having completed this phase, you reach the most crucial point of the whole assembly operation. You need to cover both the upper and the lower parts of the wings with four sheets of photo-etched material. This is a complicated task and one that needs special care, given the size of the sheet and the curvature it must be given. For this task we used bi-component glue, which takes longer to set and is more resistant, allowing us to make minor corrections. We covered both halves with adhesive, adjusted the photo-etching on the wing, covered it completely with adhesive tape, put some tiny strips of wood (the harder the better) in position and attached three or four metal clamps to exercise pressure and give the photo-etched metal the shape required. This has to be repeated four times, leaving the assembly to dry for a sufficient period each time (a minimum of 24 hours with the pressure from the clamps). Finally it remains to note that we glued all movable control surfaces on the wings in a fixed position, except the flaps that were lowered.

## Final phase

The fuselage and wings were joined together through a bolt located to the rear of the area where the wings meet and the attachment of a screw in the front part of this section. Once this had been put in place and the joints had been reinforced with liquid cyanoacrylate, we attached the central radiator, which covers the screw attachment. To complete the task we glued on the vertical and horizontal tail planes, the three cowling sections with the exhaust pipes and the five-blade propeller, which we decided to leave in a fixed position. We sanded down the hinged cabin door considerably given its excessive thickness, eliminating the central photo-etched part and adding two columns, the closing mechanism with its springs and the lever that the pilots used to bolt it.

RIGHT **The cockpit sections are pieces of vacuum-formed transparent acetate produced by Falcon and Squadron.**

FAR RIGHT **To paint the bands on the fuselage, you apply the white colour first and use masking on this to produce the black bands.**

RIGHT **A small amount of Micro Kristal-Klear was added onto the object lenses of the cameras, to obtain the correct shape for the lenses.**

FAR RIGHT **The wheels in the kit are made from resin by True Detail, and are of excellent quality.**

Before starting to paint the model, we sanded down its entire surface with the aim of eliminating any minor defects and evening out all the joins. Then we polished it with a metal scouring pad and finally cleaned it with a rag soaked in alcohol.

## Glass sections

We rejected the items that come with the model, which are vacuum-formed and not very well moulded. The central section of the cockpit canopy is completely flat whereas in reality it had a convex shape, and the rear section is too small. This obliges us to sandpaper the area on the fuselage where the third section is placed by about 2mm on each side. For the canopy we used finely moulded vacuum-formed items from Falcon and Squadron. The two rear sections are from Squadron while the front one is from Falcon, from a set that contains various World War II aircraft canopies in 1/48 scale (Set No. 3). It also includes a canopy for the earlier Spitfire PR IV, which had a similar design to that of the PR XIX.

## Wheels

These are from True Detail (ref. 46015), who have started to sell a whole series of resin aircraft wheels in 1/72 and 1/48 scale that reflect the weight of the aircraft and the effect this has upon the tyre. The quality and detail are good and we substituted these for the rubber version included with the model.

## Painting and finishing

The painting process for an aircraft made totally of metal has to be more painstaking than when we work with a plastic model. First we primed the whole surface of the aircraft with Humbrol light grey. Once this preparation had been made, we painted the invasion bands, first applying the white, and then masking it and painting on the black.

The next step was to give the whole aircraft its principal coat of PRU blue, the standard colour for British photographic reconnaissance aircraft. The Federal Standard reference number for this shade is FS-35164. This resembles Humbrol 96, Matt RAF blue, darkened slightly with black.

Before varnishing the model so as to apply the decals, we chipped off small pieces of the paint with a blade from the most worn areas. Then we applied a coat of Tamiya clear varnish and fixed the decals. Remember that, in order to help them avoid detection, RAF photographic reconnaissance aircraft did not carry roundels on the undersides of their wings. The unit codes are 2.5mm high transfers of the sort sold in stationery shops. To finish off, we added a glaze varnish and started the ageing process, producing the panelling effect with black or brown ink in the usual way.

The undercarriage wells and the internal part of the flaps were painted in grey green, like the cockpit interior. The aperture for the camera was in natural aluminium, so we decided not to paint it on our model, leaving it instead in the same colour as the photo-etched material.

BELOW **The port fuselage-mounted camera can be clearly seen here, plus the white serial codes obtained from a dry transfer set available from stationers.**

# WALKROUND

1　The Malcolm-type canopy is well displayed in this photograph of a Spitfire Mk IX.

2　The blue/green starboard wing-tip light enclosed in its fairing. Note also the panel and rivet detailing.

3　The trailing edge of each und wing radiator was movable.

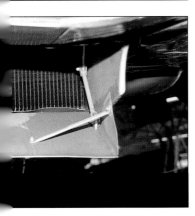

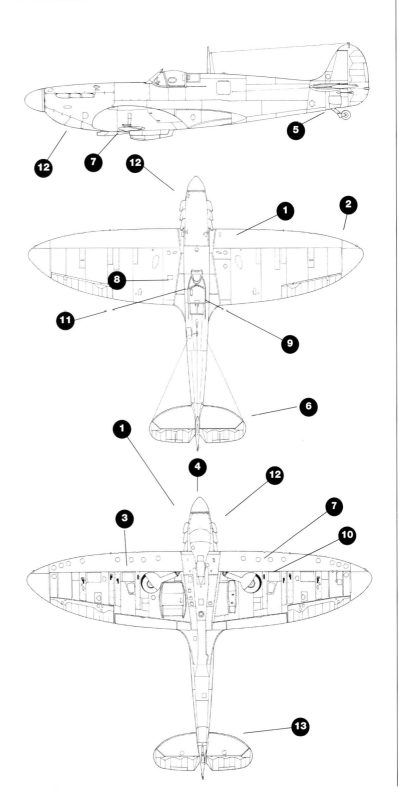

5   The fixed tail-wheel assembly. Note the angle and positioning.

4   The four-bladed propeller was introduced to the Spitfire on the Mk IX. Note also the angle of the undercarriage struts.

6   The tailplane in the drooped position. Note also the camouflage pattern and the various elements of the insignia on the tail and rear fuselage.

7   The main landing gear with hydraulic piping down the rear of each leg. The underwing radiators are also well shown.

8   The open pilot access door. Note the crow-bar is missing from the attachment in the door.

9  The Spitfire cockpit is quite cramped. Note that some aircraft carried the rear-view mirror as seen above.

10 The wheel well is quite simple, with little internal 'plumbing'.

11 The spade-shaped control column and gun sight are among the details visible here.

12 Note the six exhaust stubs typical of the later Rolls-Royce Merlin engine.

# SCALE DRAWINGS

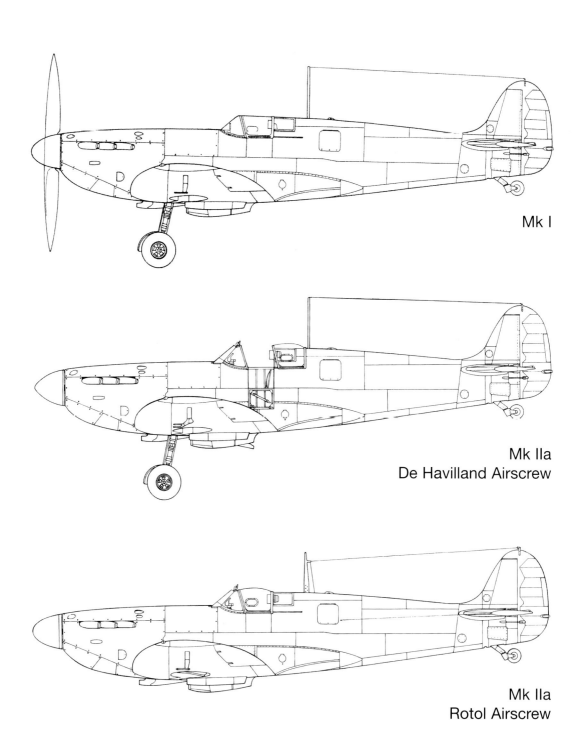

Mk I

Mk IIa
De Havilland Airscrew

Mk IIa
Rotol Airscrew

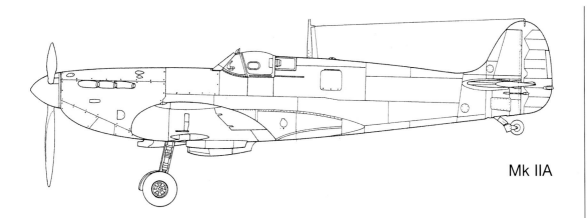

Mk IIA

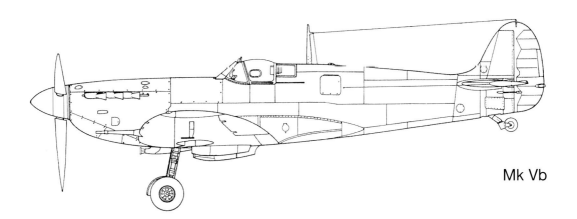

Mk Vb

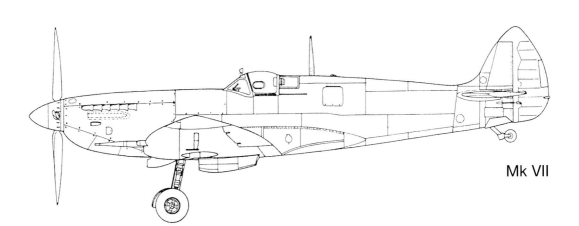

Mk VII

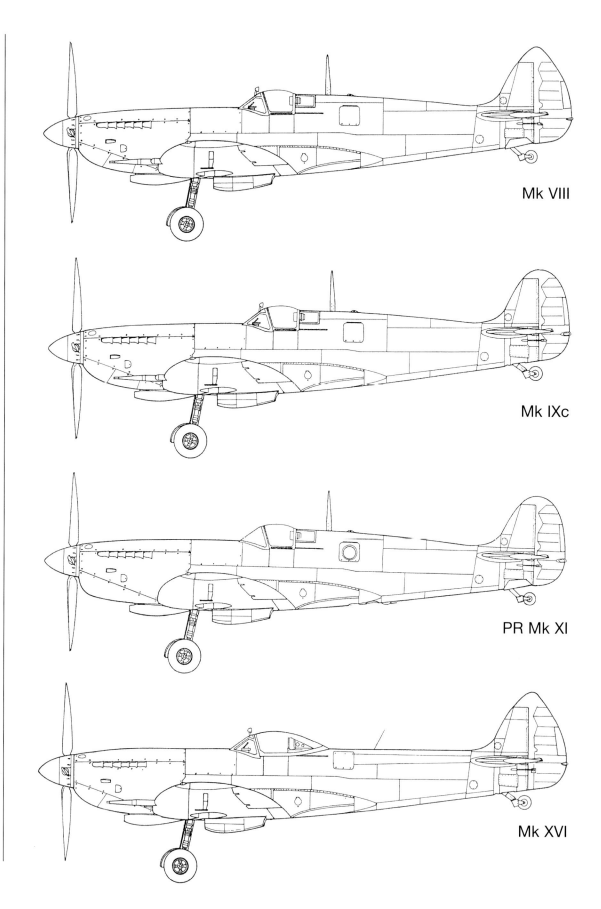

Mk VIII

Mk IXc

PR Mk XI

Mk XVI

# CAMOUFLAGE AND MARKINGS

Despite all the Orders, Rules and Regulations that required RAF aircraft to be finished and painted according to the 'Book', numerous examples exist of particular aircraft finished in non-standard schemes. Furthermore, there are many instances where non-standard roundels, code letters and personal insignia were applied not only to Spitfires but all other types as well. Some of these camouflage schemes and markings are highlighted in this text but you are strongly recommended to dig a little deeper and consult your own references. Several of the texts that we have found key to our research are listed in the references chapter at the end of this book and so we urge you to consider these early on as part of your modelling preparation.

Initially Spitfire Mk Is entered service with the upper surfaces painted dark earth and dark green. The spinner was black and between 24 April 1939 and 11 June 1940 the under-surfaces were: port wing underside night black; starboard main wing white. The under-sides of the remainder of the aircraft (nose, rear fuselage and tailplanes) were bare duralumin or silver dope. Stencil data on the night black surfaces were white. The dark earth and dark green camouflage tended to differ between aircraft whose serials ended in odd and even numbers. These were known as the 'A' and 'B' schemes. The 'B' scheme was a mirror-image of the 'A' scheme – the 'A' scheme being applied to aircraft with an even serial number and the 'B' to those with an odd serial number. These two schemes were used until 1940 but from 1941 the aircraft camouflage was standardised around the 'A' scheme, but of course, as always, there were exceptions so do check your references and photographic records for an individual Spitfire finish.

From June 1940 the under-sides were painted sky (a kind of duck-egg green colour). Under wing A-type roundels (50-inch) were painted onto these lower surfaces of the main wings. B-type roundels (40in) were carried on top of the wings in 1939 and 1940. Type A1 fuselage roundels (49in) were carried on the fuselage sides from 1940. These were very noticeable because of their

BELOW **Spitfire Mk I of No. 601 Squadron, as of June 1940, showing the standard camouflage pattern. Note the large fuselage roundel with broad yellow border. The thick bullet-proof windscreen can also be seen.**

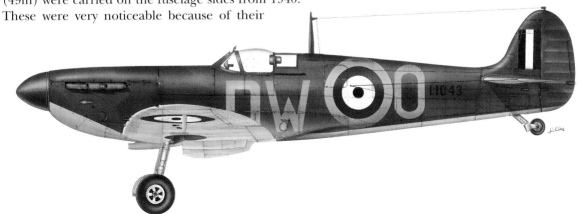

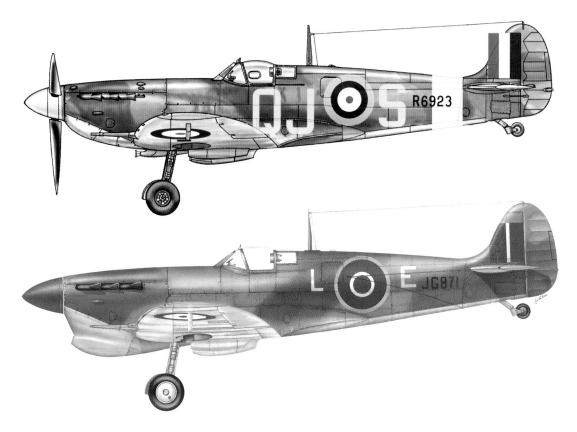

**TOP** The Mk V featured a number of changes from the earlier Mks I and II: new engine, ocean grey camouflage instead of dark earth, and new wing armament.

**ABOVE** A Mk Vc Trop of No. 871 Squadron, based in Malta in February 1943. This aircraft is unusual because of the small size of the squadron lettering on the fuselage side. Note, too, the flatter wheel-hub fairing on the main wheels and the large Vokes dust filter chin-mounted beneath the nose.

large size and distinctive broad yellow border. Squadron code letters were painted in medium sea grey.

From August 1941, ocean grey replaced dark earth on the upper surfaces for aircraft operating in the European Theatre. The under surfaces painted sky as above, were briefly changed for about five months, with the lower port wing painted night again in November 1940. Also, to help the national roundel markings stand out against the night background, they had a yellow border added. This under-surface scheme did not last long and on 15 August 1941, the under surfaces began to be painted in medium sea grey to go with the change from dark earth to ocean grey on the upper surfaces. The fuselage code letters changed from grey to sky. Another significant addition was the introduction of yellow leading edges to the outboard wing sections. Sky spinners and fuselage bands were also added. The main underwing roundels were also changed to 32in diameter C-type in May 1942 and stayed that way until 1947, well after the end of WWII. The fuselage roundels also changed at this time to 36in diameter type C1s, a style retained throughout the remainder of the war.

In complete contrast, Photo Reconnaissance (PR) Spitfires tended to be painted PRU blue overall, although early examples appeared in a rather garish pink colour. Once again, it is extremely important to check your references relating to any specific Spitfire you wish to model. The references given in this book will considerably help – especially the fine *Aero Detail Guide No.8* on the Supermarine Spitfire Mks I-V and the same company's Griffon-powered Spitfires release.

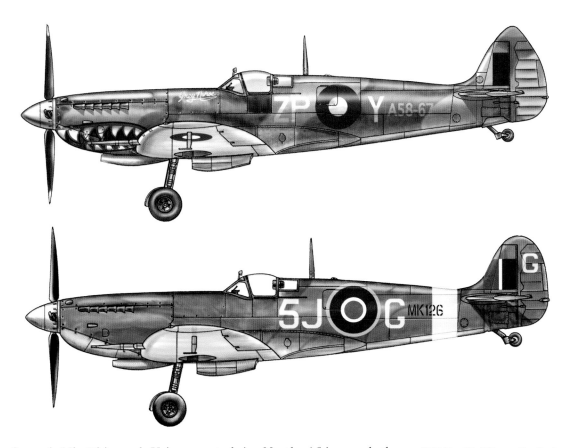

Several Mk Vb's and Vc's operated in North Africa and the Mediterranean. A famous LF Mk Vb Trop s/n AB502 is often shown in colour wartime photographs. The aircraft code is IR*G and Ian R. Gleed piloted it when he commanded No. 244 Sqn. The aircraft is typically camouflaged with dark earth and middle stone upper surfaces and light/dark Mediterranean blue under surfaces. All demarcation lines are hard-edged. The spinner on Gleed's aircraft was painted red and the aircraft featured clipped wings. The personal insignia of Wing Cdr. Gleed – 'Figaro' the cat – was painted on the starboard side of the cockpit. These Mk Vb's mainly had the 'Aboukir' filter fitted beneath the nose. Many of the North African Mk Vc Trop Spitfires were similarly camouflaged to the Vb's described above. Those such as AN*T s/n BR195 of No. 417 Sqn (RCAF) based in Sicily in the summer of 1943 had the pronounced Vokes Multi-Vee dust filter fitted and white fuselage code letters.

There has been a great deal of discussion over the years by historians and modellers about the so-called hard edge versus soft or feathered edge issue. The debate remains topical and it is worth passing brief comment here in order to help the modeller make his or her own decision. Mats were supplied for the purpose of providing a template over which the maintenance personnel could spray the appropriate camouflage colours. Unsurprisingly, then, Spitfires mainly featured hard-edge camouflage patterns. Having said this, as the war moved on, more and more pictures show that some aircraft received a soft edge to their camouflage pattern, in whole or in part. We can speculate on the

TOP **The Mk VIII was the first Spitfire type to feature the more pointed broad-chord rudder.**

ABOVE **With the introduction of the Mk IX, the RAF finally had a weapon capable of tackling the menacing Fw 190.**

**57**

ABOVE **The PR XIX sported an overall camouflage scheme of PRU blue. The national insignia were low visibility red/blue. Note the interesting positioning of the control surfaces on this model, making for a much more appealing presentation.**

reasons: crews in the field needing to get some camouflage pattern on, quickly, so that the aircraft concerned could return to operational duties as soon as possible? Some Spitfires were sprayed free hand, obviously without the mats or templates being readily available – due to attacks and damaged facilities? Whatever the reasons, look at the evidence – the photographs – and see for yourself. As we have said before – he who says 'never' and 'always' runs a dicey road!

At the time of the Normandy landings in June 1944, all Allied aircraft operating over the area were ordered to have black and white 'D-Day stripes' painted over and below the wings and around the fuselage. Many different aircraft types were so marked, including many Spitfires like the Mk IXc's of No. 312 (Czech) Sqn. In fact, because the stripes were so conspicuous, they tended to be removed from the upper wing surfaces fairly quickly. These 'Invasion' stripes should not be confused with the black and white stripes applied to some late Mk 22/24 Spitfires operating on the outskirts of the Korean War much later on.

Again, some of the late mark Spitfire F. 22s moved away from their familiar camouflaged appearance. Those serving, for example, with No. 1 Squadron, Rhodesian Air Force, out of Salisbury Airport had an overall aluminium finish and sported Type D roundels in all positions. The spinners were also aluminium. This overall 'natural metal' finish was also common on clipped-wing Spitfire Mk XIVs operated by the Belgian Air Force to whom 132 examples were supplied in the late 1940s. Belgium's was not the only foreign air force to operate the Spitfire, with Holland, Sweden and the Republic of Ireland amongst the other overseas users.

# MODEL ROUNDUP

**KIT AVAILABILITY**
This chapter describes the kits and other items that are available in the UK at the time of writing. Manufacturers and distributors, however, alter their ranges regularly, deleting some items, issuing new ones and making formerly discontinued products available once again.

Unfortunately this means that the kits used to produce the models described in the earlier chapters of this book may not be available by the time the book is published. These chapters should therefore be understood as describing general techniques, rather than giving instructions on building specific models.

Modellers who see particular kits they may need for future projects will often do best to buy them whenever they can afford to do so to ensure that they will have them available when they are wanted.

The table overleaf sets out to provide you with a comprehensive listing of the complete Spitfire kits that are available in the UK at the time of writing. We have done our best to ensure that nothing has been missed but inevitably, with an aircraft as popular as the Spitfire, it is always possible to overlook something. Several manufacturers have 'promised' 'new' items for the coming year, but many of these have been ignored because we have been frequently let down in the past – promises do not always turn into reality.

There are clearly many sources where these products can be obtained, both inside and outside the UK, with modellers increasingly turning to the Internet for suppliers across the world, as well as traditional mail-order companies at home and local model shops. Contact details for various suppliers are given in the next chapter.

The most common Supermarine Spitfire variants such as the Mk I, II and V are all well represented in the major scales: 1/72, 1/48 and 1/32. Even the small 1/144 scale has a few kits available. All of the major kit manufacturers have Spitfire aircraft types represented within their range. However, it is important to check that you are actually getting an original product if this is what you want. Several pairs of manufacturers such as Revell/Hasegawa, Monogram/Revell, Airfix/Otaki, or Italeri/Dragon have arrangements where kit mouldings appear under each other's labels and therefore what you appear to see may not be what you actually get. Asking your mail-order supplier or model shop or even the manufacturer direct will invariably clarify the position.

## ACCESSORY AND DETAILING SETS

Many accessories are available for the 1/72 scale modeller. This will certainly please those working in this smaller scale Equally, resin and etched parts have appeared for the Hasegawa Spitfire in 1/32 scale – the conversion of the Mk Vb kit into the early Prototype, for example – and from Waldron for the large Airfix Spitfire Mk Ia in 1/24th scale. Especially in these large scales, the final model can be greatly enhanced by using these products. There is a huge variety of decals available for Spitfire modellers and to list them here is impossible, given the limitations on space. There can be no substitute for getting hold of the mail order catalogues from people like Hannants and other suppliers and seeking out that interesting colour scheme you are after. Better still, take a visit

BELOW **The superb Tamiya Mk I Spitfire in 1/48 scale. The overall shape and level of detail are outstanding.**

## Complete kits by manufacturer

| | Mk I | Mk II | Mk V | PR Mk IV | Mk VIII/ Mk IX | Mk XIV | PR Mk XIX | Mk 21 | F 22/24 | Other Spitfires |
|---|---|---|---|---|---|---|---|---|---|---|
| Academy ** G | | | | | 7 4 | | | | | |
| AIM ** G ** A | | | | | | | | | | Gift set |
| Airfix ** G | 2 7 | | 7 4 2 | | 7 4 | | | | 4 | |
| Fujimi ** A D | | | | | | 7 | 7 | | | |
| Hasegawa ** A | 7 | | 3 4 | | 7 4 | | | | | 4 |
| Heller ** G | | | | | | | | | | 7 |
| ICM ** G | | | | | 4 | | | | | |
| Italeri ** A | | | 7 | | 7 | | | | | |
| KP ** G | | | | | 7 | | | | | |
| Matchbox ** G | | | | | 7 | | | | | |
| Minicraft ** G | | | M | | | | | | | |
| Monogram ** G | | 4 | | | | | | | | |
| MPM ** G | | | | | 4 | | | | | |
| Occidental ** G? | | | | | 4 | | | | | |
| PM Kits ** G | | | 7 | | | | | | | 7 |
| Revell/Monogram ** G | 3 | 3 | 7 | | | | | | | 7 |
| SMER ** G | | | 7 | | | | | | | 7 |
| Tamiya ** A | 7 4 | | 4 | | | | | | | |
| Ventura ** G | | | | | 7 | | | | 7 | 7 |

**Key**

7=1/72 scale; 4=1/48; 3=1/32; 2=1/24; M=other scale D=discontinued

**Skill Level and Accuracy Guide:**

*** = For modellers experienced in using resin/etched metal   ** = Limited level of skill required

A = Accurate   G = Generally accurate

to any good model shop and browse through the different manufacturers' products and try their websites, too.

We have listed below just some of the manufacturers of resin, etched metal and other conversion items/accessories that are currently available, together with an indication of the kind of products they offer the Supermarine Spitfire modeller. The following conventions are used: skill level and accuracy needed: *** = for modellers experienced in using resin/etched metal, ** = limited level of skill required; A = accurate, G = generally accurate

**Aeroclub** *** G. Aeroclub are well known to most modellers. They produce a good range of resin accessories for the Occidental Spitfire Mk IX in particular. In addition, they also produce clear vac-form canopies and resin engines – both the Rolls Royce Merlin and Griffon.

**Airwaves** *** G. Airwaves etched metal sets are produced by E.D. Models in the UK. Most of their sets are formed from etched brass but resin accessories are now also available. There are many interesting items in their range like the different types of wing with appropriate armament. Several interesting conversions for different and unusual marks are also available. The quality of the items produced has improved over the years and now a good range of parts and accessories for Spitfire modellers is available.

**Eduard** *** G. Eduard also produce kits, but are best known for their huge range of etched metal parts. The range is simply vast and you can spend many a long hour perusing lists of what they have available. The Spitfire modeller is very well catered for with several etched sets for the Mk V, VIII, IX and XIV in particular. Among their most useful additions are the etched instrument panels with acetate dials that fit behind the main panel. The effect is excellent and very realistic. Don't forget those seat belts and harness sets, too.

**Falcon** and **Squadron** replacement canopies *** G. These canopies are vac-formed clear replacements for the kit parts. They are generally very well moulded and clear but their greatest advantage over the kit parts is their scale thickness. They are much thinner than the polystyrene kit parts and, although tricky to remove from their backing sheet, add hugely to the finished model. This is particularly the case if you want to display your model with the canopy open.

**Hi-Tech** *** G. This French company producing resin detail sets is known to many and has been established for many years. They had the reputation for setting the standard for resin parts early on. They have some items useful to the Spitfire modeller, in particular resin cockpit sets and usefully one for the Airfix F 22/24.

**Paragon** *** A. This company, founded by Neil Burkill, is renowned for the quality and variety of interesting resin conversions. There is a significant focus in the range on the 1/32 scale modeller who is largely ignored by most of the other aftermarket manufacturers.

**Reheat** *** G. Reheat probably have the leading name when it comes to instrument panels, placards and dials, and the like. Their range of etched parts is vast and it is easier to say go and look at their full listing. Their sets invariably compliment those resin detail sets that you might use from other manufacturers and are well worth investigating if you are unfamiliar with them.

**True Details** *** G. This company offers a good range of resin and etched metal cockpit parts for the Spitfire modeller. Their hallmark, however, is the range of weighted tyres that is available. They seem to have established somewhat of a niche here with very few other manufacturers offering weighted tyres. Just occasionally, the 'flats' on the tyres look a little too flat so it is always worth checking this out with your references.

**Waldron Model Products** *** A. Some excellent instrument sets are provided for those modelling the Airfix Superkits like the Mk IA. Their main additions also include seat belts, buckles and shoulder harness plus rudder pedals.

ABOVE **The recently released Mk I/II in 1/32 from Revell. The new wing is moulded with finely engraved panel lines but the original fuselage has raised panel lines. Rescribing the fuselage detail is therefore necessary.**

BELOW **Academy's quarter-scale FR Mk XIV. This is a generally well-moulded scale model. Very few kits of the Mk XIV are available in 1/48 scale so your choice is limited.**

61

# REFERENCES

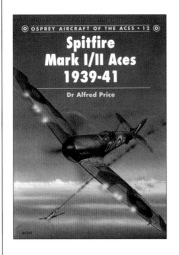

## BOOKS

Osprey's excellent **Aircraft of the Aces** series includes three useful titles: *Spitfire Mark I/II Aces 1939-41*, *Spitfire Mark V Aces 1941-45*, and *Late Mark Spitfire Aces.* These thoroughly researched volumes include good colour side profile views of different aircraft that can be used as the basis of modelling projects. By definition, the main aces' aircraft are well represented. From a modeller's perspective, they are great inspiration to go away and track down the specialist decal sheets relating to a particular ace's aircraft.

*Spitfire, Aircraft in Action No. 39*, published by Squadron Signal Publications. This book is very concise and particularly helpful in giving the detail differences between each mark of Spitfire. It also contains good line drawings and wartime photographs that truly show the weathered state operational Spitfires got into.

*The Great Book of WWII Airplanes*, published by Crescent Books. A truly awesome reference work by any standards. The Supermarine Spitfire is just one of the aircraft featured but the quality of the line-drawings and cutaway colour profiles gives much to the Spitfire modeller.

*Aero Details Guide No. 8, Vickers Supermarine Spitfire Mks I-V*, and *Guide No. 30 Griffon-Powered Spitfires*, published by Dai Nippon Kaiga Co, Japan. This series of books could be summed up as 'nice-but-expensive'. They are designed specifically with the detail scale modeller in mind. This guide has everything you could want: quality colour close up photographs of surviving examples of the type, scale plans, line drawings and detailed information on camouflage and markings.

*Wings of Fame*, Vols. 5, 9 and 16, published by Aerospace Publishing. These volumes in the current series deal in detail with the Supermarine Spitfire. They are particularly interesting for the quality of the period colour photographs and colour profiles. A succinct text accompanies the large number of photographs and some interesting colour schemes and individual aircraft are featured.

## MUSEUMS

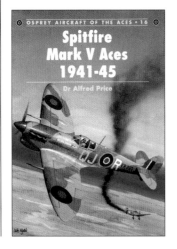

The museums and organisations listed below normally have Spitfires of the various marks and serial numbers noted on display, though it is always wise to check beforehand if making a special journey as exhibitions change from time to time.

**Battle of Britain Memorial Flight Visitors Centre**, RAF Coningsby, Lincolnshire: Mk IIa P7350, Mk Vb AB919, Mk IX MK356, PR XIX PM631, PR XIX PS915.

**Dumfries and Galloway Aviation Museum**, Dumfries: Mk IIa P7540.

**Fleet Air Arm Museum**, Yeovilton, Somerset: Seafire F. 17 SX137.

**Hall of Aviation**, Southampton, Hampshire: F. 24 PK683.

**Hurricane and Spitfire Memorial Building**, London (Manston) Airport, Kent: Mk XVI TB752.

**Imperial War Museum, Duxford**, Cambridgeshire: F. 24 VN485.

**Aircraft Restoration Company/British Aerial Museum** (also based at Duxford): Mk Vb BM597.

**The Fighter Collection** (also based at Duxford): Mk V EP120; Mk IX ML417; Mk XIV MV293; F.22 PK624.

**Old Flying Machine Company** (also based at Duxford): Mk IX MH434.

Other operators based at Duxford have a Mk Vb BM597 and a Tr IX ML407.

**Imperial War Museum, London:** Mk I R6915.

**Museum of Flight**, East Fortune, Scotland: Mk XVI TE462 and F. 21 LA198.

**Museum of Science and Industry in Manchester:** FR XIV MT847.

**Potteries Museum and Art Gallery**, Stoke-on-Trent, Staffordshire: Mk XVI RW388.

**Real Aeroplane Museum**, Breighton Aerodrome, East Yorkshire: PR.XI PL965.

**Royal Air Force Museum**, **Hendon**, London: Mk I K9942, Mk I X4590, Mk Vb BL614, F.24 PK724.

**Royal Air Force Museum**, **Cosford**, Shropshire: Mk XVI RW393.

**Shuttleworth Collection**, Old Warden Park, Bedfordshire: Mk V AR501.

# WEBSITES AND USEFUL ADDRESSES

Hyperscale (**www.hyperscale.com**) is excellent for build articles and technical information/reviews. An information request service is available, too, through other users of the site.

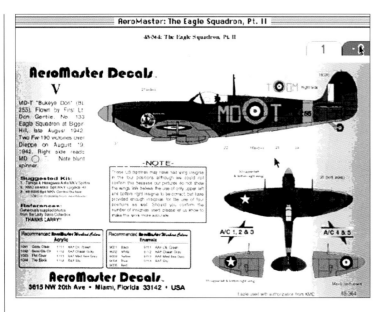

The **International Plastic Modellers Society** has a wide network of branches and special interest groups throughout the world. Membership of the British section of the society also brings access to The IPMS (UK) Modelling Weekend each year plus many regional shows organised by the various local branches. A Technical Advisory service and member's Decal Bank are also features. If you require further information you should contact the Membership Administrator: Sue Allen, 8 Oakwood Close, Stenson Fields, Derby DE24 3ET; www.users.globalnet.co.uk/~ipmsuk.

ABOVE **Websites help manufacturers and suppliers give full details of their products so that you can be sure what you are getting when you buy online or by mail order. At the AeroMaster site, for example, you can view exactly what each decal set includes.**

BELOW **Meteor Productions' website gives details of the Cutting Edge Modelworks accessory sets, like this one for the Spitfire F. 22/24.**

# STOCKISTS

One of the best stockists, with just about everything for the modeller is **Hannants**, Harbour Road, Oulton Broad, Lowestoft, Suffolk, NR32 3LZ, England; tel: 01502 517444; fax: 01502 500521; www.hannants.co.uk. Also well worth noting are **Historex Agents**, the UK distributor of Verlinden products, Wellington House, 157 Snargate Street, Dover, Kent, CT17 9BZ, England; tel: 01304 206720; fax: 01304 204528; email: sales@historex-agents.demon.co.uk. Another good stockist/mail order source is **The Aviation Hobby Shop**, 4 Horton Parade, Horton Road, West Drayton, Middlesex UB7 8EA, England; tel: 01895 442123; fax: 01895 421412.

Hannants also stocks a wide range of accessories from many makers including the excellent **AeroMaster** decals (you can contact the company at www.aeromaster.com); **Eagle Editions** a specialist reference/decal supplier (also at www.eagle-editions.com), and **Cutting Edge Modelworks/Meteor Productions** for resin, etched items and decals (also at www.meteorprod.com). **Airwaves** brass and etched metal items can be obtained from E.D. Models, 64 Stratford Road, Shirley, Solihull, B90 3LP, England; tel: 0121 744 7488; fax: 0121 733 2591; or email: airwaves@ultramail.co.uk.

**Midland Counties Publications** is an excellent specialist book supplier: Unit 3, Maizefield, Hinckley, Leics. LE10 1YF; tel: 01455 233747; e-mail: midlandbooks@compuserve.com.

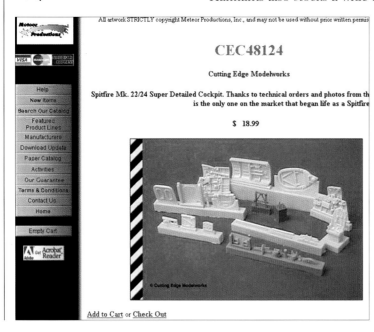